Speak to THAT MOUNTAIN

Carol Davidson

Speak to That Mountain

ISBN: 978-1639457175 (sc)
ISBN: 978-1639457182 (e)

Writers' Branding
1-877-608-6550
www.writersbranding.com
media@writersbranding.com

Contents

About the Author

Carol Davidson wrote *Speak to That Mountain* during a painful time in her life when she was searching for healing and peace. She went through forty-two years of abuse, and therapy wasn't enough. She needed an outlet. Through the Holy Spirit, God gave to her revelation on how to teach others to be released from their bondages of pain, fear, resentment, and hate. She teaches others how to become victorious over their circumstances, to love themselves, and to find that peace they so desperately need.

Speak to That Mountain is a teaching, healing, and mentoring book. She describes how to deal with abuse. Through the Word of God it teaches you to forgive, to be set free, and build your faith so you can be an overcomer of anything that comes your way. Victory is yours when you speak to your mountain.

Introduction

I look back on my life and think about how I can help others who have experienced the same pitfalls that I have; how to help others understand that things that happened to them were not their fault. They were just victims of their circumstances.

I was sixty years old as of writing this, and I wanted to share what I have learned over the span of my life. You may have been a victim, but you can become a victor. You shall have your victory; you only need to seek the right source. God always sees our plight and hears our pleas, though we do not always hear Him. Ask God to open your ears to hear Him, and block any hindrances so you can receive what He has in store for you. It takes faith and trust, but the Word of God was given to us to take authority over all things for our own good.

Mark 11:23–24 tells us that Jesus said, "For verily I say unto you, that whosoever shall say unto this mountain, be thou removed, and be thou cast into the sea and shall not doubt in his heart, but shall believe that those things which he saith shall come to pass; he shall have whatsoever he saith. Therefore I say unto you, what things so ever ye desire, when ye pray, believe that ye receive them, and ye shall have them."

You cannot receive what God has for you if you don't ask. You cannot have all that belongs to you if you do not believe. What can you believe in? For starters, you can believe in peace, love, health, hope, and happiness for yourself. Why not? You are only held back by your lack of belief.

If thou canst believe, all
things are possible to him that
believeth.

Mark 9:23

Abuse Is More Than Improper Treatment

What is abuse? Abuse is, by definition, improper treatment. It can be verbal, emotional, mental, or physical. To a person who is currently or has been abused, abuse means pain, torture, betrayal, belittlement, and fear. You can have sympathy for someone who's been abused, but you don't have any idea what it's like unless you've experienced it for yourself.

Abuse is degrading; it strips away your self-esteem. You feel unloved and, worse, unlovable—so much so that you can no longer reach out to express love, for fear of being hurt. It puts you in a glass bubble. You can see and hear what's going on around you, but all of the toxic emotions you feel won't let you break out of your mental confinement. You can't trust. You feel like Pavlov's dog, always expecting the abuse to happen again. So you emotionally draw back into a shell to protect yourself.

Some people refuse to remember their abuse because they cannot bear to face it. They have blocked out the memories in order to deal with the reality of their pain. However, it shows in their physical and mental health and the way in which they live their everyday lives. Some people become ill from the effects of the abuse. Some may require medication, counseling, or both. Some are so depressed they wish they were dead and even commit suicide.

If you are a victim of abuse, find someone you can trust and tell that person about what is happening to you now or what has happened in your past. You need to seek help. Find a professional therapist and, if necessary, a medical doctor to see if you need medication. Everyone is different; the level, duration, and how you have dealt with your abuse will determine what you need to recover.

Some people think they are coping with their abuse and don't see the negative impact it has on their lives. That was me. I went through forty-two years of abuse thinking I could handle it on my own, but I was wrong. I couldn't see how it was affecting me. Even though I had so much negativity in my thinking, I thought my way of dealing with my life and emotions was normal. I was not coping with the pain. I hid it, buried it away.

I couldn't have a happy life. I pretended that I was happy and that everything was fine, but I could barely laugh. I wanted to, but I felt that part of me had been blocked off. I held so much resentment, anger, fear, pain, distrust, and insecurity bottled up inside of me. It's hard to laugh when you carry such a burden. I felt like crying, but I kept it buried deep inside me, thinking that crying meant showing weakness. I didn't have a way to relieve my stress or pain.

Most abusers are controllers. They get you to the point of submission, and then they use that power to control you. I felt like a puppet being yanked to and fro. High demands were made of me, but little was given in return.

Most abusers have negative mind-sets. They speak highly of themselves, needing to build up their egos, and then they belittle other people because of their own low self-esteem. Many of them were raised in abusive households. Either they were abused themselves or they saw the abuse of other family members, creating a cycle of abuse. They do not see anything wrong with it; they are only emulating what they know as reality.

They need help as well, but sadly, they do not realize it. They are full of doubt, distrust, fear, pain, feelings of inferiority, and resentment. They have no inner peace, so there is only strife around them. Sadly, they are also victims of circumstance.

My Confession

I bind the spirit of depression and loose the spirit of joy. I bind all hindering spirits and loose ministering angels about me right now, in Jesus' name. "Whatsoever thou shalt bind on earth shall be bound in heaven: and whatsoever thou shalt loose on earth shall be loosed in heaven" (Matthew 16:19).

Now take the time to write your own confession.

Seek to Forgive

You could have been abused by a spouse, parent, relative, or a complete stranger. You may have been a child or an adult. I can tell you from my own experience, after all that you have been through and as hard as it may sound, you have to *forgive.*

You say, "What? You mean after all they put me through, I have to be the one to forgive?" *Yes*! But I'm not saying it will be easy or that you can just forgive right now. "Let all bitterness, and wrath and anger and clamor and evil speaking, be put away from you, with all malice" (Ephesians 4:31).

When you do not forgive, you remain in bondage to the person who has harmed you. He or she is still controlling your life, your thoughts, and your feelings. You are not free; you are in a self-created prison. When I finally did forgive the one who abused me, I felt the release of my spirit; I didn't feel the gnawing resentment inside me anymore. I wasn't able to forgive right away, though. I thought I had forgiven, but the anger crept back up inside me when I remembered the awful pain.

I felt rejected, unloved, and lonely because I was too embarrassed to tell anyone. I was afraid that the person who abused me would lie or that others would think my abuse was my own fault. But God says in Isaiah 41:10, "Fear thou not; for I am with thee: be not dismayed; for I am your God: I will *strengthen* thee; yea, I will *help* thee; yea, I will *uphold* thee with the right hand of my righteousness" (emphases added).

Naturally, your abuser isn't going to admit to what he or she has done, as that would be admitting guilt. He doesn't want to lose the control over you that gives him power. She will hold you in bondage so you can't get free. The Devil wants you bound, not free. "The thief cometh not but for to steal, to kill, and to destroy" (John 10:10).

The Devil turned the situation around and told me that I deserved to be mistreated, that it was entirely my fault. *That's a lie!* He tried to steal my peace and destroy me by making me feel unlovable and undeserving. *That's another lie!* We *do* deserve to be loved and respected. I am worth it. So are you!

I asked God to help me to forgive. You should do this as well for anyone who has hurt or harmed you in any way. Let go of all the thoughts of the past, or you'll just keep reliving all the old memories and the pain. Believe me, I have done this too.

Don't keep needlessly suffering on the same roller coaster of emotions. Don't keep bringing up the past with your words, and don't rehearse them in your mind. The Devil will keep attacking your mind to try to weaken it with painful thoughts to keep you from receiving peace and healing, but you have a sound mind. "For God hath not given us a spirit of fear; but of *power*, and of *love*, and of a *sound mind*" (2 Timothy 1:7, emphases added).

My Confession

I confess that I have the power of God's Word, that fear does not dominate me, that I am redeemed out of the hand of the Enemy, and that the Devil has no authority over me. "No weapon that is formed against thee shall prosper; and every tongue that shall rise against thee in judgment thou shalt condemn" (Isaiah 54:17).

Now take the time to write your own confession.

Be Set Free with Your Words

To forgive, first you have to make a conscious effort to say, "I forgive that person." Secondly, you have to forgive him from your mind and then from your heart. To forgive is a decision, but letting go of the pain and resentment—healing—is a process. When you do you will cease to feel hostility toward your abuser. This is not something you can do overnight. You have to let go of the tremendous burden you are carrying. Otherwise, you will succumb to an endless cycle of pain from which you are never set free. Do you want to be set free?

"Thou shalt decree a thing, and it shall be established unto thee" (Job 22:28). So I decree that I have forgiven. I decree that I have courage and strength. I decree that I am set free from all hostile feelings. "If the son shall make you free, ye shall be free indeed" (John 8:36).

If ever you feel you can't do it, call upon God for strength, and remember this Scripture: "But I can do all things through Christ which strengthened me" (Philippians 4:13). You may say, "But I can't go on." Remember this Scripture: "My grace is sufficient for thee: for my strength is made perfect in weakness" (2 Corinthians 12:9).

How is His strength made perfect? His strength is made perfect in our weaknesses. We cry out to Him and speak His Word, which strengthens us. That reinforces His Word and makes it strong in us. Therefore, we rely on His Word to meet all our needs.

You are not free and will never be set free if your thoughts haunt you. By holding on to resentment, do you think you are getting even? It doesn't hurt your abuser at all when you keep rehashing your anger with painful memories. So what good is it to hang on to the resentment? Speak God's Word over in your mind. "Thou wilt keep him in perfect peace, whose mind is stayed on thee" (Isaiah 26:3).

You have to say, "Enough is enough. It's time to let go of the past." Go on with your life, and be set free. The Devil loves to see you miserable and will keep flooding your mind with confusion, doubt, pain, and fear. With a resentful spirit you will lose the battle. Resentment makes you weak, full of pain, and defeated. It deepens wounds and sets you up for endless suffering. You build a cage of mental confinement with your negative thoughts and words. You never break out of that confused confinement; you only rattle your cage with your words of pain and resentment. So you strengthen the bars of your cage with strongholds that you've built with your words of anger. Anger is a poison that will confine you.

So, is it better to hold blame and want to get even? Let it go and be set free! The anger comes from pain; the depression comes from the pain. Get rid of the pain, and you have the peace. The problem is: how do you get rid of the pain? There's no peace in revenge, only in forgiveness and love. You have to make a conscious effort to say, "I'm not going to think that or say that anymore." Start speaking to that mountain of pain. Build strongholds in your healing with the words you speak. You will break that source of negative confinement.

In Matthew 11:28, Jesus invites us saying, "Come unto me, all ye that labor and are heavy laden, and I will give you rest." God will take your burden from you, and you will have peace beyond all understanding. You have a battle, but you are not alone.

He hath delivered my soul in
peace from the battle that was
against me.

Psalm 55:18

My Confession

I confess that I have a renewed confidence working in me, for greater is He that is in me, than he that is in the world. I release forgiveness into my spirit right now in Jesus' mighty name.

And when ye stand praying,
forgive, if ye have aught against
any:

that your father also which is
in heaven may forgive you your
trespasses.

Mark 11:25

Now take the time to write your own confession.

Make Peace with Your Enemies

And having made peace through the blood of His cross, by Him to reconcile all things unto Himself.

Colossians 1:20

God says He wants us to reconcile and have peaceful relationships. That does not mean that you have to be in love with the one who abused you, but you must release forgiveness to him or her.

You are only required to love God, but you must show compassion to everyone, including the person who hurt you. How do you know when you have truly forgiven someone? You start to feel the peace. Or, as stated in Matthew 12:34b, "For out of the abundance of the heart the mouth speaketh." Do you still resent what they did?

When it's hard to forgive someone, your confession shows what's in your heart. Are you speaking condemning, despising, or saying hateful words? Or are you speaking forgiveness, peace, and mercy?

Luke 23:34 tells us that at a time when He was nailed to the cross, lied about, hated, and beaten, Jesus bade, "Father forgive them; for they know not what they do." He still asked for His abusers to be forgiven. He walked in the spirit of love. We should not have unforgiving hearts; it robs us of the blessings of God.

Proverbs 12:18 tells us, "There is that speaketh like the piercings [*stabs*] of a sword: but the tongue of the wise is health." When you speak ill of your abuser, not only are you cursing that person with your words, but you take on the curse also. That is made very clear in Mathew 12:36–37, which states, "But I say unto you, that every idle word that men shall speak, they shall give account thereof in the Day of Judgment. For by thy words thou shalt be ye justified, and by thy words thou shalt be condemned." That means any words you speak bring judgment, good or bad. What are you speaking? Are the Word of God and the love of God spoken through you, or do you speak the hate-filled words of the Devil?

Speaking hateful, despising words curses your abuser and yourself. Conversely, Romans 12:14 teaches us to "bless them which persecute you: bless, and curse not." Likewise, Colossians 3:13 bids, "Forbearing one another, and forgiving one another, if any man have a quarrel against any: even as Christ forgave you, so also do ye."

God teaches us forgiveness with His Word so that unforgiveness does not confine us to living in sin. God commands us to love our enemies and pray for them. He teaches us, "Death and life are in the power of the tongue: And they that love it shall eat the fruit thereof" (Proverbs 18:21).

You should not go around speaking words of condemnation about anyone—not a neighbor, a friend, a relative, or even an acquaintance. Words are very powerful. Your words create something every time you speak. If you speak blaming, anguishing, or disparaging words, you sow hate and bitterness into your life with those words. You could even end up like the person who abused you. By using hate-filled or condemning words, you can take on the same spirit and fall into the same condemning trap.

My Confession

I confess that there shall be peace in my house. I confess I will not speak words of condemnation, and the words that I speak will not burden but lift up.

And my people shall dwell in
a peaceable habitation and in
sure dwellings, and quiet resting
places.

Isaiah 32:18

Now take the time to write your own confession.

Chapter 5

Speak Power into Your Life

Be strong and of good courage,
fear not, nor be afraid of them:
for the Lord thy God,

He it is that doth go with thee;
He will not fail thee, nor forsake
thee.

Deuteronomy 31:6

Praise God, we're not alone! To have victory in your life you have to begin to profess the Word of God. You set boundaries for your life with your words. You can and will establish the will of God in your life with the words you speak. Get into the Word every day; it's the burden-removing, yoke-destroying Word that brings healing, deliverance, and prosperity to manifest in your life. However you have to speak it into your life—take authority. What do you need right now? Speak it!

The Devil may tell you that you deserved your abuse; that, after all, no one likes you and you're not good enough. These are lies from the Devil! Don't listen to the words of the Devil.

> So then faith cometh by hearing
> and hearing by the Word of God.
>
> Romans 10:17

You are only limited by what you believe. Ask what you will, and it shall be done unto you. God's promises are as close to you as getting them in your mouth and speaking them into your heart.

One evening God spoke to me while I was preparing dinner. He said "Speak to that mountain." So I spoke Mark 11:23, "That whosoever shall say unto this mountain, be thou removed, and be thou cast into the sea; and shall not doubt in his heart, but shall believe that those things which he saith shall come to pass; he shall have whatsoever he saith."

I took authority over my mountain and started speaking to my mind and to my spirit that the Word of God is established in me. I can do all things through Christ Jesus. What is a mountain? A mountain is any obstacle that keeps you from receiving the will of God. There can be many mountains in your lifetime, such as your finances, your health, your marital problems, et cetera. My mountain was abuse.

God is a god of love; He meets all our needs. We only need to seek Him, ask Him, and then believe He will do what He says. Hebrews 10:23 confirms this by saying, "Let us hold fast the profession of our faith without wavering; (for He is faithful that promised;)."

God can't move until you release His Word into your life. He is faithful to His Word, not to words of doubt or unbelief from the Devil. God said to speak to that mountain, so speak to that pain. Tell it to go, and receive your healing. Speak to that fear, rebuke it, and receive your peace. Speak strength to your spirit.

But they that wait upon the Lord
shall renew their strength.

Isaiah 40:31

What causes Jesus to work miracles in us and for us? Faith, believing God will keep His word to us, worshipping Him, and putting our faith into action. If you doubt the Word of God, you won't receive His promises.

For with God nothing shall be
impossible.

Luke 1:37

My Confession

I confess that my ears only hear that which comes out of the mouth of my Master, my God, my Abba Father. I speak redemption into my life right now. I'm set free.

Let the redeemed of the Lord
say so, whom He hath redeemed
from the hand of the enemy.

Psalm 107:2

Now take the time to write your own confession.

Your Faith Makes You an Overcomer

To overcome the pain of abuse, you have to talk with God every day. Then profess His word concerning your situation and walk in faith. Build your faith.

> And calleth those things which
> be not as though they were.
>
> Romans 4:17b

Believe that those things you speak are true, and they will manifest in your life. However it takes constant effort to keep His Word before your eyes and to speak it every day.

Live it, drink it in, and it will become so real and so tangible that you can actually feel the Word of God manifest in your body. It happened to me. It was such a glorious experience. I was speaking God's Word over my life one day, and all of a sudden, I felt it filling my body. It was a burst of power. It started in my abdomen, like a birthing. It spread through my body, and I knew that the Holy Spirit had just filled my spirit with His Word. I felt such peace, and I knew that I had overcome my mountain.

It's not really as hard as it sounds. What do you choose to believe for in your life, victory or defeat? I have fought the Devil to get my mind and my life back. Take authority, and speak to your mountain, saying, "I am the righteousness of God. I am the victor. I am an overcomer." You will be what you believe. Keep the faith!

Now faith is the substance of
things hoped for, the evidence of
things not seen.

Hebrews 11:1

You will have forgiveness for the abuser, and don't forget forgiveness for yourself. Don't beat yourself over the head, because you could have done this or you could have done that. You can't change the past, but you can change the present. Only look at what you can change now. The future will change as you change.

I have learned to have faith, trust God, forgive, speak love, show love, make peace, take authority over the Devil, and receive healing. Through God's Word there is only victory. Father God, I ask that You establish Your will in my life. I'm supposed to be a witness.

Whenever the Devil comes in to attack me, I put up the shield of faith to break his strongholds with the Word of God. I resist letting his negative words come out of my mouth and prevent his negative thoughts from coming into my mind. He wants me to believe that I'll never overcome the pain in order to keep me so weak that I can't be a blessing so that I can't receive my healing, so I can't be a witness. Instead, I establish words of faith in my life.

Our words are weapons we use by faith to bring things to pass. No enemy can stand before you, because your faith will absolutely defeat the Devil in every battle.

The enemy encamps around you to put negative thoughts into your mind to cause you strife, envy, jealousy, resentment, pain, poverty, sickness, loneliness, and death.

> Casting down imaginations, and
> every high thing that exalteth
> itself against the knowledge of
> God, and bringing into captivity
> every thought to the obedience
> of Christ.
>
> 2 Corinthians 10:5

Do you want a breakthrough? How do you do that? You have to penetrate the enemy's camp with worship—*just worship*! You will have victory! God never said that you wouldn't go through any tribulation. He said you wouldn't go through it alone. Confess His Word every day.

The words that have grown out of faith in your heart will continually bring you victory and break the power of demons and heal the sick. We learn in Hebrews 13:15 that "by Him therefore let us offer the sacrifice of praise to God continually, that is, the fruit of our lips giving thanks to His name."

My Confession

I confess that I have unshakable faith, I have courage to move forward with the power of God's Word, and I have full restoration of spirit, soul, and body.

And they overcame him by the
blood of the Lamb, and by the
word of their testimony.

Revelations 12:11

Now take the time to write your own confession.

God's Unfailing Love

"Tell My people about Me! I'm as close as that smoke you put in your lungs or that bottle you put in your hands. You're looking for silver and gold, but you can't find Me! You scratch, but you only scratch each other. Tell My people about Me!"

This is a recent word that I received from God, who is deeply concerned about you. You either belong to Him or to the Devil. God doesn't want you tormented, sick, broke, or lacking in any good thing.

How can you find Him when you're not looking in the right place? How can you find Him when you don't ask? How can you find Him when you're looking in the wrong direction? How can you find

Him? Just call out His name: Jesus, Jesus, Jesus! He's been waiting for you. God's love is given to us continually. Even when we don't love Him, He already loves us.

We need to see ourselves as God sees us. God sees us as His children. He sees us forgiven. He sees us set free. He sees us victorious. He sees us redeemed. He sees us healed. He sees us as a new creation. He sees us righteous. He sees us prosperous. Once you receive Jesus as Lord and Savior, all these things become real in your life.

Not too long ago God said this to me, "There is a difference between earthly human love and godly (Holy) love." His people are limited by what they believe love is. He is unlimited as He is love.

Let us look at perfect love:

Love is patient and kind:

We will not complain, and we will be thoughtful

of others.

Love is not jealous:

We are not envious of anyone or anyone's possessions.

Love is not boastful or proud:

We will be humble and won't feel we are better than anyone else.

Love is not rude:

We will show respect and not be impolite.

Love does not demand its own way:

We will not control people or circumstances.

Love is not irritable:

We will not be easily annoyed or be ill tempered.

Love keeps no record when it has been wronged:

We will not bring up the past about a person's sin.

Love is never glad about an injustice:

We will not be happy when someone is falsely

accused.

Love never gives up:

We can always be there for someone.

Love never loses faith:

Our faith will never waiver.

Love endures through every circumstance:

We will stand firm on every position.

When we walk in love, nothing evil can attach itself to us or block what God has intended for us because we do not open the door to the Devil. It's easy to walk in love. Showing love to God is simple. You love Him by loving others. You love Him by fellowshipping with Him. You love Him by keeping His commandments. You love Him by staying in His Word. You love Him by forgiving others.

Because love forgives, because love heals, because love protects, because love gives unconditionally, love doesn't ask for anything in return. Love picks us up when we fall down. Love fills the emptiness in us. Love sacrifices for us. When you release love into any situation, you have released God into it.

The Holy Spirit has been touching you and God has been showing you things, but all of a sudden you let things block them out. But God says if you will put Him first in your life, He will lift you up. The Holy Spirit wants you to develop your senses to recognize when God is doing something in your life. We need to say to God, "Show me, teach me, I don't want to miss You." Throughout your life, God wants you to believe with all your heart and speak with your mouth all that you are in Christ Jesus.

Many people fail to receive what they pray for because of they don't understand confession. Confession is simply believing God's promises in your heart and repeating them with your own lips. What you confess is your expression of your faith. Confession comes from your heart. You are to stand firm in your confession of what Christ has done for you. Believe in Christ the Redeemer, the Advocate, the Savior, the healer, the provider, the protector, the teacher, and the blessings never end.

> And the Word was made flesh, and dwelt among us, (and we beheld His glory as of the only begotten of the Father,) full of grace and truth.
>
> John 1:14

Jesus is the Word, the Word in the flesh. He lived it, He spoke it, and He walked in it. Every time you speak the Word of God you are being filled with Jesus. Jesus is looking for someone who will accept Him and love Him. You have Jesus' heart, but does He have yours.

Many people have been taught that they have to be holy to get God's attention. No, He's not looking for holy people. He's looking for hungry people, hungry for Him and His word.

Come to Jesus today, and receive Him and His love and the blessings that He wants to give to you. It's a promise that will be fulfilled; you just have to ask.

If you would like to ask Jesus to become your Lord and Savior, or if you just want to rededicate your life to the Lord, just say out loud this simple prayer:

> Jesus, I believe You are the Son of God. I believe You died and rose again. I repent of all my sins. I receive You now as my Lord and Savior. Thank You for coming into my heart and being the Lord of my life.

When you say that simple prayer you become the righteousness of God, born again, child of the almighty God! You are now heir to the promises of God. Jesus is the same yesterday, today, and forever. He never changes. His grace, mercy, and compassion will belong to you.

Your faith is being restored

right now!

Your peace is returning

right now!

The victory is yours

right now!

Now speak it!

Now believe it!

Now receive it!

In Jesus' mighty name

it's yours!

Mark 11:23–24

Mark 9:23

Matthew 16:19

Ephesians 4:31

Isaiah 41:10

John 10:10

2 Timothy 1:7

Isaiah 54:17

Job 22:28

John 8:36

Philippians 4:13

2 Corinthians 12:9

Isaiah 26:3

Matthew 11:28

Psalm 55:18

Mark 11:25

Colossians 1:20

Matthew 12:34b

Luke 23:34

Proverbs 12:18

Matthew 12:36–37

Romans 12:14

Colossians 3:13

Proverbs 18:21

Isaiah 32:18

Deuteronomy 31:6

Romans 10:17

Mark 11:23

Hebrews 10:23

Isaiah 40:31

Luke 1:37

Psalm 107:2

Romans 4:17b

Hebrews 11:1

2 Corinthians 10:5

Hebrews 13:15

Revelations 12:11

John 1:14

www.ingramcontent.com/pod-product-compliance
Ingram Content Group UK Ltd.
Pitfield, Milton Keynes, MK11 3LW, UK
UKHW040013200726
13854UKWH00001B/184